From Orangutan to Rocket Scientist

How to Lead and Engage Your Team Through Effective Process

Ryan Weiss

First Edition Design Publishing
Sarasota, Florida USA

From Orangutan to Rocket Scientist

ISBN 978-1506-907-21-5 PBK

LCCN 2022901104

January 2022

Published and Distributed by
First Edition Design Publishing, Inc.
P.O. Box 17646, Sarasota, FL 34276-3217
www.firsteditiondesignpublishing.com

Table of Contents

Introduction

On the journey in life, we have been impacted by many people and ideas. When compiled into a cohesive model, these can transform the way you think and ultimately create value for others. The purpose of this book is to share a number of stories with questions for you to reflect on around your organization's Purpose, Product, Performance, People, and Process (the P^5 Rocket).

You will also gain access to several simple, but powerful templates that have helped numerous business leaders to align and focus teams to drive success.

There are 3 key points that you, the reader, will want to keep in mind as you read the pages of this book.

1. *"Clearly aligned processes enable your team to optimize performance and ultimately fulfill your organization's purpose"*

2. *"Process without People is Waste and People without Process are Frustrated"*

3. *"In order to grow, your team must possess the Tools, Skills, and Mindset!"*

Most of my clients have experienced one of these conditions:

- *Rapid growth has outpaced your processes*

- *Misaligned departments or teams has led to frustrated and disengaged employees*

If you have a team that is frustrated and disengaged (and many are today), then this book will provide you with ways to increase the engagement and energy of your team to propel your **P^5 Rocket**™ in the right direction with incredible energy!

Chapter 1

What can we learn from an Orangutan?

While visiting the Henry Doorly Zoo in Omaha with my wife and children, I read a story about an orangutan that had lived there in the 1960's. After reading the sign, I was struck by the similarities between the story of the orangutan and the challenges facing many organizations in their journey to improve.

The head zookeeper at the time was becoming very frustrated by the carelessness of his staff. Over the course of time, the orangutans had been escaping the confines of their cages, presumably because someone was carelessly leaving them unlocked.

He had almost reached the point of firing someone to "send a message" when one of his employees observed something spectacular… The employee raced to find the zookeeper, and they watched in amazement as the lock was picked, the door was opened, and the orangutans escaped.

The story reminded me of a slide I used in training classes when teaching about making process improvements. At the time, it was the most uninteresting slide in the deck, and I struggled to bring it to life.

The slide looked something like this:

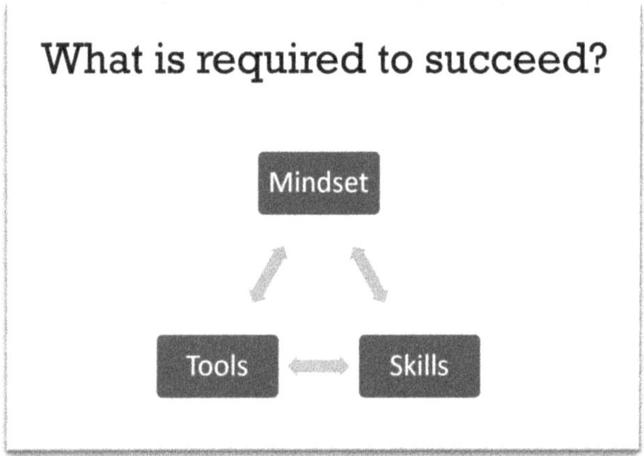

This was one of those moments in life where the picture became so clear, as these were exactly the three things the orangutan **required** for his escape as well…

1. A **tool** to pick the lock.

2. The **skill** to figure it out.
3. The **mindset** to escape!

If the orangutan was unable to overcome any one of the requirements, he would have to stay within the confines of his cage, and never escape. It turns out that all these characteristics are also necessary for making any organizational improvement. Lacking any one of them will keep us in the cage of doing things the way we always have.

We are reminded of the tongue-in-cheek definition of insanity: to repeat the same thing over and over, while expecting a different result. If we want a different result, we need to first uncover which of the three requirements are deficient, and then work to improve in those areas.

The story of the orangutan leaves us with a several questions...

- Where did he get the **tools** from?
- Did an employee **give** him a key?
- Where did he get the **skills** from?
- Did someone **give** him training?
- Why did he **desire** to get out of the cage?

It would not be so spectacular if we learned that someone had given a key to the orangutan and trained him in lock picking. What is more amazing is that **he chose** to get out of the cage, and then worked diligently to obtain the tools and teach himself the necessary skills. He did not sit back and complain about not having the right tools or needing some training that his manager would not give him.

After rounding up the orangutans, the employees proceeded to examine "Fu Manchu" in order to find his "key". What they found shocked them. He was hiding a length of wire along his gum line so that it would not be easily discovered in routine examinations!

We can learn a lot from the orangutan...

He was not born with the skills. These were learned.
He was not given the tools. They were obtained.
He was not forced from the cage. He chose to get out.

The orangutan had what it took to make a change to improve his process... He had a mindset to obtain the tools and learn to use them to get out of his cage!

The goal of this book is to provide you with a new set of tools to align your team, optimize their processes, and develop life transforming leadership skills for success. The mindset to move forward will be up to you!

The next several chapters will provide you with the model for success, including templates to develop and practice the requisite skills. Are you ready to eliminate pain, reduce risks, and enhance your success?

Then welcome to the journey!

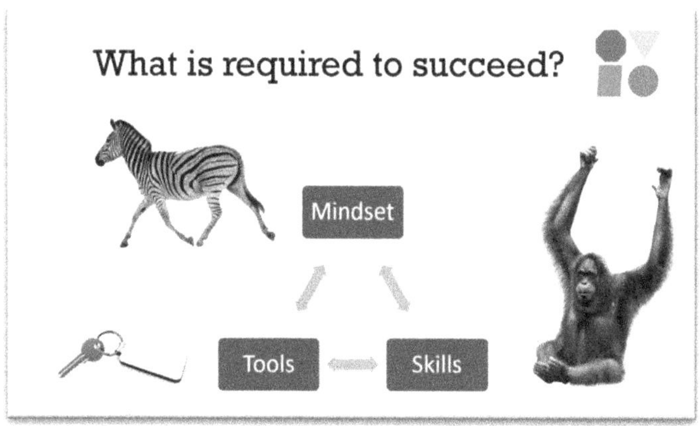

Chapter 2

Intro to the P5 Rocket™ Strategy

Have you ever wondered why some organizations fly efficiently and effectively and others crash and burn?

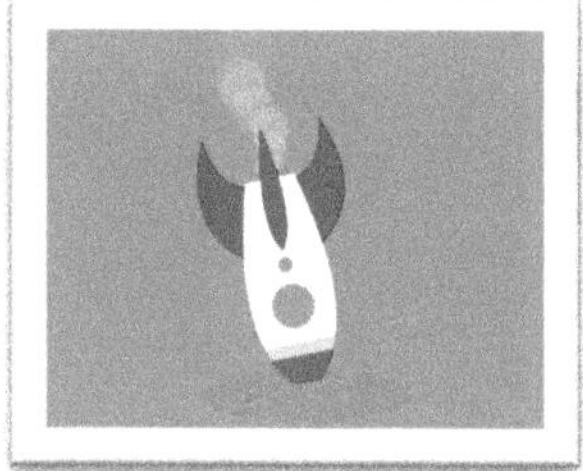

The answer lies in the P^5 Rocket... You will learn that each of the components is important of its own accord, but when optimized in combination, true transformation happens.

The components of the rocket include:

Purpose: Your vision for the future. Where do you want your organization to go and why?
Product: What value your organization provide to clients today and why?

Performance: How do you measure performance on your path from where you are today to where you want to go in the future?

People: Who is your leadership team, and do you have the right people in the right seats?

Process: How effective and efficient are your processes in supporting your team?

Human Energy: How engaged and energized are your employees in propelling your organization toward your compelling vision of the future?

"Clearly aligned processes enable your team to optimize performance to ultimately fulfil your organization's purpose."
-Ryan Weiss

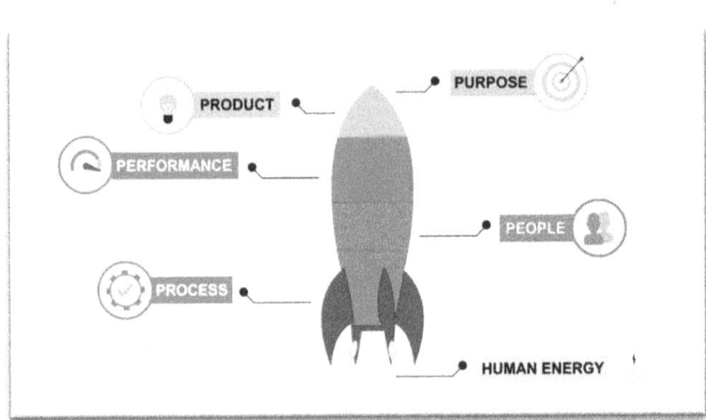

For an organization to be extremely high performing, it requires that all of these elements work cohesively together

Lack of common purpose leads to resistance and severely restricts your organization from reaching your destination. If you don't know where you are going, and why it is important to get there, then it will be incredibly difficult for your team to imagine on their own. Setting vision and purpose are core functions of leadership. These are not tasks that can be delegated or pushed aside. Leaders must set the course and engage our teams to grow together with common purpose!

Product is a subset of your organization's purpose when it is defined in the following way:
Your product is the value you create for customers that compels them to buy from you.

Why is your "product" important to your clients? Why have you chosen to create value for your clients with the product or service that you provide today?

The product or service that you provide today is your current state. The vision you have for where you want to go is your future state. The gap between current and future state enables creation of your roadmap to success!

Outlining your customer's journey is an outstanding method of articulating the value that you create and the gaps that exist in your pursuit of excellence.

Lack of performance metrics and alignment makes it incredibly difficult to validate where you are at and to confirm that you're on course to get where you want your organization to go.

Imagine for a moment being on a rocket with no idea of where you are currently at. If you are unable to articulate your current state purpose and product, then it will be very difficult to ensure that you are pointing in the right direction.

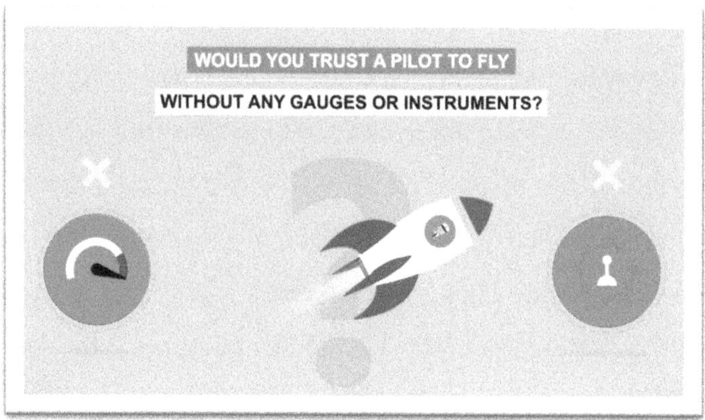

The other gauges that you need indicate the direction, speed, and other vital information that leadership needs to make wise decisions to course correct as needed.

If different departments have metrics that are misaligned with each other, this can cause confusion amongst leadership, which flows throughout your organization.

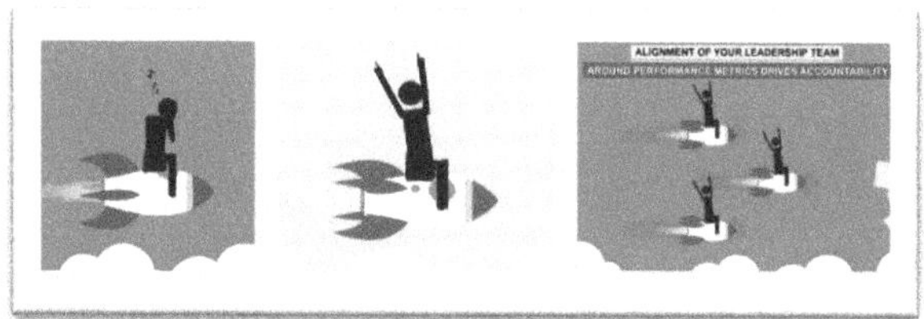

Are all your leadership seats filled with the right people focused on a common goal?

In business school we were taught that the purpose of a board was to maximize shareholder value. As I have gained experience, I have come to understand that this can mean different things to different individuals and organizations. Maximizing value for a non-profit is very different than maximizing value for a for-profit entity. A shared purpose with common values becomes essential to your organization's success!

In order to be successful, you must identify why you do the things you do. Answering this question will help you define what maximizing your team's efforts looks like.

Clear Optimized Processes Enable Your Team to Drive Performance and Fulfill Your Organization's Purpose. Which of your processes are restricting your organization from reaching its full potential?

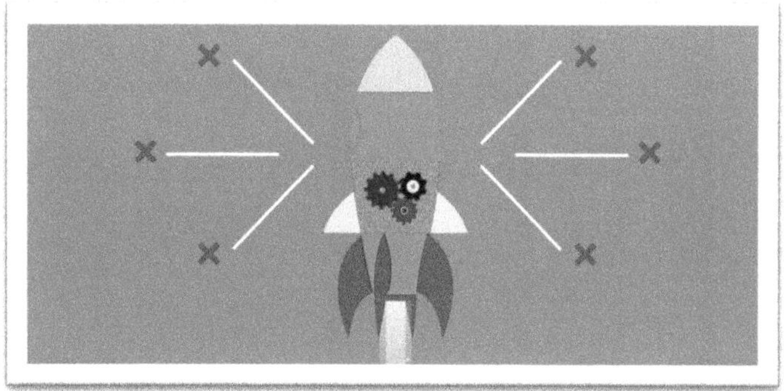

Ultimately, the human energy of your organization propels it forward and controls your velocity. Which represents your team's human energy?

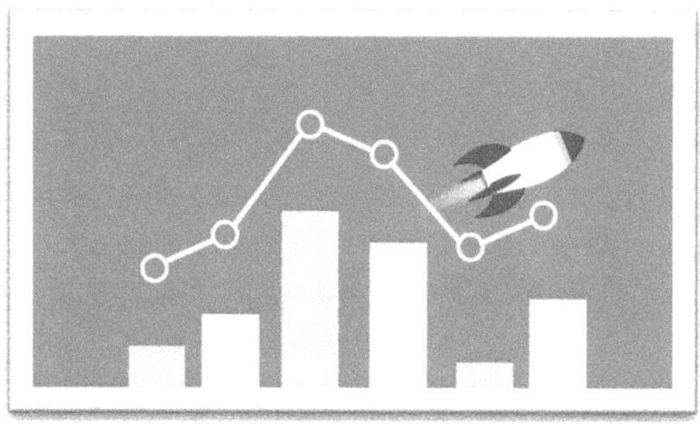

In the next chapters you will gain a deeper perspective about each of the components, and how they fit together. You will also be posed with questions and challenges to alleviate pain, minimize risks, and dramatically improve the profitability of your organization. We will start from the bottom of the rocket (Process) and work our way to the top (Purpose).

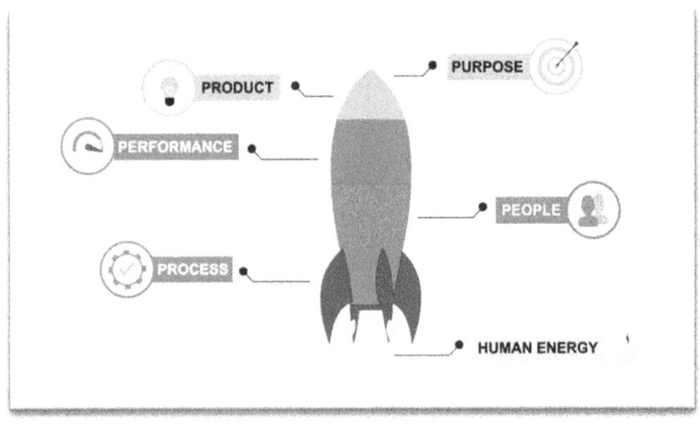

"Clearly aligned processes enable your team to optimize performance to ultimately fulfil your organization's purpose."

-Ryan Weiss

Chapter 3

Great Leaders Understand the Importance of Processes

Well aligned processes enable your team to optimize performance, and ultimately fulfill your organization's purpose. Process is not the most important element of the P5 Rocket, but if it is not functioning well, it will dramatically impact every other element.

Consider this key difference between managers and leaders:

- Managers *"manage people to a process"*
- Leaders *"engage teams to improve processes"*

Process is the underlying enabler of success for your team and organization! Without solid processes, your team will become frustrated, ineffective, and inefficient.

Relationships remain a critical component in both leadership and sales. It has been said that all things being equal, people will buy from people they like. All things not being equal, they will still buy from people they like. This is still true today. Customers and employees must like us, trust us, and respect us. One of the key components of respect is that the customer must believe that we understand their business, their pain, and what keeps them up at night.

It was exactly this realization early in my career which led me to the understanding that the Voice of the Customer's Process™ would be applicable to nearly every business process, in nearly every industry. I have since applied the concept across a wide variety of processes and industries with great success.

Many new innovations were essentially created to address process problems such as:

- Ketchup bottles are now upside down to eliminate the various process 'tricks' diners used to extract ketchup, such as the angled shake, the bottom tap, and the vigorous shake to squirt.

- Automobile hands free phone systems attempt to reduce distractions of drivers, and manufacturers are working feverishly to make autonomous cars, to eliminate the human process entirely.
- A single device now holds our music, directs us to unknown destinations, organizes our life, and facilitates communication, among other things.
- Many exercise gimmicks sold on TV attempt to make the workout process 'easier' while still delivering results.
- Parents now give small toddlers pouches of baby food which they can handle on their own… A very different process compared to using small spoons to scoop, tempt, insert, wipe, clean, repeat!

It is important for now to understand that every organization has customers, and those customers have processes. The goal for businesses is to understand the voice of your customer's process, and fill identified needs to gain sustainable advantages over competitors.

A few questions you should ask to get started:

- Who is your customer? (Internal or External)
- What is their process? (*This is not the same as "What do you think your customer does?")
- Have you observed your customer's process? (Translated: Have you ever built a process map with the individual or team about their process?)

- How does your product or service impact their process? (Start with the customer perspective, not your internal view…)
- Do you recognize the value of your product/service? (As perceived by their point view…)
- How could you impact their process in a more positive way?

(After answering the questions above - What products/ services do you have to offer? Better yet, what could you offer?)

One example that I personally experienced of this concept in action was a waitress who observed my process. She saw that I used the French Vanilla cream in my coffee during a business breakfast. More French Vanilla cream containers appeared without my asking. She didn't ask what type of creamer I wanted, she didn't do a survey of which creamer her customers preferred, and she didn't do an internal cost analysis of the optimum number of creamers to put on the table. She instinctively understood the voice of her customer's process by observing my process and reacting with outstanding customer service.

There are a number of reasons I start our process discussion focused on your customer's process first. Self-focused processes often lead to sub-optimal results. Focusing your

team first on your customer's process enables alignment of your team around a common goal of value creation!
Quite simply put, "process" is a sequence of steps that transform inputs into outputs. Processes exist literally everywhere in life, regardless of whether you define them or allow them to define you!

An additional area of research that you will find particularly useful in seeking to improve your ability to lead through process is the observation of habits. Understanding the influence of habits, and how they control people's decision making (both internal and external), is critical to identifying what you can do to positively impact your customer's experience, and your employees' engagement.

All habits follow a predefined cycle: Cue-Process-Reward. As you grow your leadership skills, I encourage you to observe the people around you, and the processes that they follow. This observation should include your customers, employees, leadership team, and self-reflection. Three questions you should ask are:

- Do you understand the individual's cue?
- Have you observed the process they follow?
- Do you understand the reward they experience?

As you reflect on these questions, the answers will enable you to dramatically improve your ability to engage your team in creating processes of efficiency and effectivity.

Great leaders and organizations ensure that their core processes are documented and followed by all. A CEO I have known for decades had always indicated that he felt his organization's processes were solid. He recently called me when he lost a key employee and found himself investing a huge amount of time training the replacement employee. None of the processes were documented well enough to onboard and develop the new employee in the key role.

What key process gaps might you have in your organization that either cause you pain, leave you open to risk, or have potential for improved efficiency or quality?

Distractions – even minor ones – make a dramatic impact on the efficiency and effectivity of process. In the course of observing hundreds of processes around the world in manufacturing, transactional, and service industries I have found that even tiny distractions have a major impact.

Take the example of searching for a specific sized wrench as an example. I once observed a 20-minute activity that resulted in nearly 2 hours of machine downtime. The 20 minutes included a machine operator needing to mechanically adjust some settings on the equipment in order for the high-speed process to function properly.

About 10 minutes into the adjustments, the operator had to stop to search for the correct size wrench to make an adjustment. As he walked around searching for the correct tool, he became distracted by some mess that he straightened out, some paperwork that needed to be completed, labels that needed printing, and a pallet that needed to be moved.

The first minor distraction (looking for the correct size wrench) turned into many other distractions. When he finally made it back to the machine, he had actually forgotten about the wrench! He continued making other adjustments, and started the machine at a jogging speed.

Unfortunately, as he had forgotten the final adjustment, the process did not proceed as planned... He spent the next 45 minutes troubleshooting the problem, until remembering which setting, he had forgotten to finish!

This is not a unique situation. I actually have observed this similar situation over and over again. Before you think that this is unique to manufacturing... When was the last time you were in the middle of a profound thought, and your cell phone buzzed? When was the last time you were in the zone creating a presentation, and your email notification popped up? When was the last time someone was telling you something they felt was very important, and you glanced at your watch when a new text arrived?

We live in a distracted society. Clear and simple processes are more critical now than ever before!

Reflection Questions About Process

1. Why is it important for you to solidify processes between departments and throughout your organization?

2. How many of your core processes are clearly document-ted and followed by all?

3. What steps will you commit to taking in order to close any gaps that exist in your current processes?

Chapter 4

Alignment of People and Processes is Essential to Driving Effectivity and Efficiency

Many consultants tend to focus more heavily on either People (DISC, PI, and MBTI) or Process (Lean, Six Sigma, TPM).

What we have found is that the true magic lies between the two – The intersection of People and Process

Processes without People => Waste.

People without Process => Frustrated.

Training people to communicate effectively, without equipping them with tools to solve the root causes, leads to ongoing frustration.

Likewise, process without engagement of people leads to wasted efforts. I have observed teams spend countless hours on "perfect technical processes", only to have them never implemented... One of my early career managers named George had a simple, but wise, saying: "Don't let the perfect stand in the way of the good." In effect, he was teaching us not to hold too tightly to perfect processes at the expense of getting buy-in and support for implementation of a better process than the one we currently had.

Imagine being an astronaut trying to communicate with flight control, without clearly defined responsibilities and processes! I recently read an article about the top 3 personality traits NASA looks for:

- A thick skin
- A long fuse
- An optimistic outlook

Even if the astronauts and engineers have all been carefully selected and coached around personality styles and communication styles, there will be incredible frustration when met with the challenges of ineffective processes.

I recently met with a CEO who informed me that the problem in his organization was that people lacked the mindset that I talked about in chapter 1. I carefully asked the follow up question – Did you hire the people with that mindset, or did they become that way over time?

You see, as W. Edwards Deming (pioneer of process improvement and quality) once said:

"A bad process will beat a good person every time."

Another mentor, Joe Slawek offered a great perspective in his book the 14 Ingredients in Success and Life:

Seek Excellence, Not Perfection.

When people seek perfection, they almost never get it. This leads to frustration, arguments, and frequently inaction. Pushing ourselves and our teams to pursue excellence leads to exponentially better outcomes. Excellence is both achievable and motivational! When we get buy-in from others that leads us in a common direction, great things happen.

If you have never mapped out your customer's process on a map, how can you confidently state that you know what these are? It is likely that your team is overlooking key challenges that your customer has, because of a simple concept:

We see things not as they are, but as we are...

Suppliers see all of their customer's problems through their own lens of being a 'plastic manufacturer' or a 'paper supplier', or an 'ink supplier'. In other words, all of the customer's challenges must be solvable with a change to the ingredient you sell.

This is not really the way that customers work.

Customers see their challenges through a different lens. They see their challenges as something they want to solve. They may prefer if you solve it because of a long-standing relationship, but in the end, they are more concerned about their pain, then your solution.

Imagine engaging a customer in applying tools to better understand, refine, and prioritize their pain points in a way to innovate together about solving their problem.

How would your relationship change with your customer's if they viewed you as a resource to solve their problems, rather than a vendor they purchase from?

The most powerful way to align different departments around a common process is to make the common thread the customer's process journey that we explored in chapter 4.

Departments can often focus on their own processes in order to optimize for themselves. A very effective way to ensure alignment between departments is to link all of them to the common goal of providing effective and efficient service for the client.

The best tool we have found to enable the documentation of processes is a combination of creating a SIPOC (will be explained later), with a tool called the Job Breakdown.

Job Breakdowns are different from the Standard Operating Procedures (SOPs) implemented by most companies. SOPs often articulate in great deal "what" to do and "how" to do it, but they miss a critical element... "the reason why".

I learned about the Job Breakdown several years ago, and quickly began to understand the wisdom in including the "why" behind each process step.

My favorite example is when a restaurant manager I was working with told me that he had an employee "Robert" who was incapable of consistently performing the simple task of "flattening the protein".

I asked Aaron to explain a bit more:

- Was Robert capable of knowing what to do? Aaron replied, Yes! I have told him many times to perform the task.
- Was Robert capable of knowing how to do it? Aaron replied, Yes! All he has to do is use the meat tenderizer to flatten the chicken breast.
- Does Robert know why it is important to flatten the protein? Aaron replied, no, he would look like a deer in headlights if we asked him why.

After this discussion, I gave Aaron a simple challenge to complete the following week:

1. Show Robert why it is important (quite simply, the sliders they make are hard to eat if the chicken breast is too thick).
2. Have Robert repeat back, and demonstrate how hard it is to eat a slider if the chicken breast is too thick.

What was the outcome of this experiment? For months afterwards, I asked Aaron several times if Robert was consistently flattening the protein. His response? **Every. Single. Time.**

It is important to recognize that Robert was capable of following the directions, and performing the task consistently, once he connected the "why".

It has been proven that employees are trained more than 25% more efficiently and effectively when they are taught what, how, and why.

We also had a client's team who was concerned about the time it would take to document their processes with this method, and whether it would be worth the effort.

Below are the team's anonymous answers demonstrating the impact process documentation using this method had on their job clarity, work-life balance, stress, and being overworked.

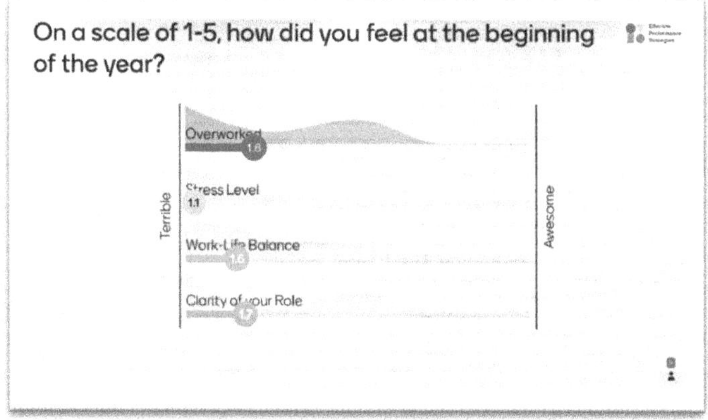

Prior to the start of the exercise, you can see they rated all of these aspects very low on the scale.

We asked the question again after completion of the process documentation exercise in which they were all involved, and were surprised to receive the following result:

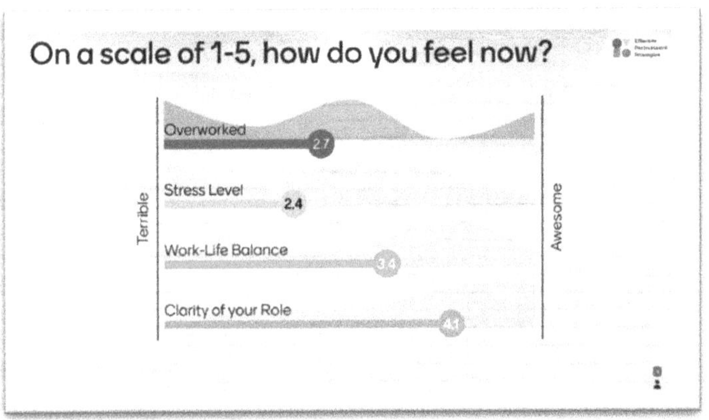

You see, the act of documenting processes in the method described dramatically improved the feelings of the employees by 2x – 3x!!

This leads us into the following chapter about Human Energy. If you can engage your team in working on the right things, they will actually become more excited about their jobs, and ultimately take better care of your clients.

In an interview with Inc. Magazine, Sir Richard Branson said the following:

"If the person who works at your company is not appreciated, they are not going to do things with a smile," Branson says. By not treating employees well, companies risk losing customers' over bad service. To this end, Branson says he has made sure that Virgin prioritizes employees first, customers second, and shareholders third. Effectively, in the end shareholders do well, the customers do better, and your staff remains happy.

-Sir Richard Branson.

Reflection Questions About Alignment

1. Why is it important for you to have alignment between people, processes, and performance metrics?

2. What gaps exist in the alignment of your people, process, and performance metrics currently?

3. What steps will you take to close these gaps and move your organization forward?

Chapter 5

Why It Is Critical to Align Teams Around Common Performance Metrics

I was moved to the Philippines in 2013 to turn around the North American shared service center operations of a major chemical company and was entrusted with a team of nearly 180 people. When I first arrived I was excited at the new opportunity, and also overwhelmed by the challenge.

After the first year into my assignment, I started having chest pains. The full impact of everything I had taken on was weighing me down. I was responsible for my wife, our children, 180 employees in Manila, and my team was growing with the addition of a global team including direct reports in Slovakia and Mexico.

Two things happened at about the same time that changed my life.

First, I set up an appointment with a Filipino doctor. I vividly recall how I felt as I walked through the hospital to his office, wondering what tests or medications he might recommend. Sadly, I don't recall his name, as I would love to share with him the impact that he had on my trajectory... The visit went something like this:

> **Doctor:** *Welcome! What brings you to my office today?*
>
> **Me:** *I have been feeling some chest pains for the past several weeks that just don't seem to be going away.*
>
> **Doctor:** *Interesting. What do you do for work? Is it stressful?*
>
> **Me:** *No, it isn't really that stressful. I have an amazing team of folks that I manage in a night shift operation. I love what I do, and the people I work with!*
>
> **Doctor:** *How much coffee do you drink?*
>
> **Me:** *Well, I drink a couple of Starbucks Americanos every night to stay awake, and I often take team members downstairs to meet at the coffee shop.*
>
> **Doctor:** *I see... How much sleep do you get?*

> ***Me:*** *That is a problem! I have trouble sleeping when I get home during the day, because I drink so much coffee to stay awake during my shift...*
>
> ***Doctor:*** *How much exercise do you get?*
>
> ***Me:*** *It is really hard to exercise, because I always feel tired, because I don't sleep, because I drink so much coffee, because of my job...*
>
> ***Doctor:*** *You seem like a smart guy - You don't need medicine – You will figure this out. So, how have you been enjoying your life here in the Philippines?*

He transitioned from leading me to the solution through a logical series of questions to casually letting me know that I was capable of figuring it out on my own!!!

I learned a lot in that moment - I needed to get my stuff together.

The second thing that happened at about the same time, was that my top manager approached me with a question. Rizza asked me: **"Boss don't you trust me?"** Those 5 words have seared into my memory like a branding iron.

Fortunately, I was aware enough to want to know why she was asking, her underlying meaning, and to react in the proper way. I sat down with her to seek where she was coming from, and the things I was doing that led her to ask the question.

Instead of leading, I had been managing.

Rizza shared with me her concerns that I was not letting her lead her team. I was trying to fix everything myself, rather than providing a framework for our leadership team to grow and succeed.

I was leading 180 people across 8 teams with very diverse processes: consumer call center, supply chain, material planning, accounts receivable, accounts payable, continuous improvement, customer service, general accounting and controlling. This created a complex challenge that needed to be figured out, and I love a good puzzle!

It was clear **we** needed to change, and that opportunity came through an idea to create a common framework applied across all of our teams on a corkboard outside of my office. This is what I now call the QVS™ framework. QVS™ stands for Quality, Value, and Speed. The next chapter will explain this in more detail, but for now you can be aware that this was life transforming for me.

One critical consideration when monitoring metrics is to confirm that the data is relevant, representative, and accurate.

At a factory in Shenzhen China, I was brought in as a "Six Sigma Expert." The meeting started with drinking tea together with the local management team in an executive's office (a local custom). They were very interested in my ability to analyze the machine downtime data that they had accumulated and wanted to get started right away.

Fortunately, one of the valuable lessons I had learned several years prior was to FIRST go and observe the process. Initially, they were more hesitant to allow me into the factory than to share data with me for analysis. However, after insisting for quite some time that I first wanted to observe the process before looking at any data, they took us out into the production area.

After observing for about 30 minutes, they asked me if I was ready to go back to the office yet. I let them know that I would like to observe for a longer period of time. After approximately 1.5 hours, we finally went back into the office.

When back in the office, they asked again whether we could review the data that they had about the machine downtime. My challenge at that point was to politely find a way to inform them that the data they had was useless. In the entire 1.5 hours that we spent observing, the machine stopped on several occasions for various reasons; however, the

computer being used to gather the data was on screensaver during the entire observation period!
After finding a polite way to point this out, we discussed a plan, and they agreed to assign individuals to record data full time for the following two weeks.

The results that were uncovered were remarkably different than the original data set and led to very different conclusions by management about the root cause of their productivity loss!

Blindly following data does not necessarily lead to successful results. First, you must understand the process, before you can implement a mutually beneficial solution. This is true for every organization I have worked with.

One particular example that I experienced that I will never forget was tampering on a massive industrial scale that showed a clear link of how simply implementing and performing quality checks on a product was actually creating more variation (poorer quality) to their end customer!

A food manufacturer had implemented a quality control test to measure solubility of a thickener and was struggling to maintain consistency for many years. After observing the manufacturing process and test method, I encouraged the team to perform a measurement system analysis, which is basically a method of checking the consistency of inspectors to consistently obtain the same result. What we found was shocking. We learned that if two different analysts blindly tested the same lot of thickener, one might find the solubility was too high, and another might claim the same material was too low! For years, the manufacturing team had been making process adjustments based on a flawed Quality Control test and had actually been increasing variability of the end product by tampering.

"Garbage In => Garbage Out" is a relevant maxim when considering using data to align your team. In order to successfully align your team towards a common purpose, it is critical to engage your team in the spirit and intention of the QVS™ system, and not simply as a measuring stick to be manipulated for people to show what they think management wants to see.

If your GPS isn't accurate, then you likely won't get where you want to go. Make sure to understand the data being collected, the incentives being used, and the accuracy of the outputs!

Imagine being on a spaceship with broken or missing instruments. How would you know where you were, and whether you are on the right path to your destination? The anxiety would be intense, and it would build over time. The same thing happens within your team as they look around at unclear metrics and direction, or when they distrust the information being used to make decisions.

Here is some Biblical wisdom to consider as you contemplate metrics, motivation, and purpose:

> *So whether you eat or drink or whatever you do, do it all for the glory of God,* (1 Corinthians 10:31).

Do the right things for the right reasons. Integrity and quality will pay dividends far beyond the financial benefits that many business leaders seek.

People are motivated by different things in life. Tapping into their motivations is critical to engaging and aligning your team around a common purpose. Purpose is the focus for alignment. How you measure and ensure alignment is up to you and your team to develop together, and will be explored further in the next chapter.

Reflection Questions About Performance

1. What anxieties or frustrations are you feeling that will require a change of mindset to solve?

2. What data are you collecting or relying on currently that may be misleading?

3. What gaps do you have in your organization that could be closed through a system of alignment?

Chapter 6

Driving Accountability by Transferring Ownership to Your Leadership Team Through QVS™

There were 3 critical elements of success with the implementation of what I now call QVS™.

1. The teams had to select their own metrics and results to enhance ownership
2. The teams had to create habits around monitoring and improving the metrics
3. The teams had to have the authority to act, without fear of repercussions.

All three of these are important for different reasons, and I have observed others fail in execution by missing the purpose behind each.

My leadership team needed to be accountable for their respective teams to improve my health, and to enhance the employee engagement for us to win together. This required me delegating with a level of trust. I asked my continuous improvement manager Cherry to decorate a cork board outside my office with a matrix, as you can see in the image below.

I then requested each manager to identify 3 relevant metrics within their department. One for quality, one for value (or cost), and one for speed (or timeliness). These 3 metrics had to be relevant to their process, and something they wanted to improve.

There was some hesitation and resistance as we worked through this first step together. They were accustomed to being "told" which metrics that they should focus on. The problem was that we had hundreds, if not thousands, to choose from. We were overwhelmed with data and choice!

I held the line and convinced our leadership team that they needed to select the metrics with their teams. It was critical for me that they own what they chose to improve. After all, they were closest to their processes.

They knew what their problems were.
They knew which metrics their team struggled with.

My requirement was that they needed to select metrics in each category that met the following criteria:

1. **Opportunity for improvement.** *Don't give me a metric that is 100% every month already. That is a waste of time*

2. **Relevant to process pain.** *I don't want to know how many coffees your team drinks*

3. **Quantifiable on a monthly basis.** *The cork board would need to be updated by each team monthly.*

This led us to the second element of success: The teams had to create habits around monitoring and improving the metrics.

Each month, each team was responsible for doing the following: Print out their updated metrics, and post them on the board, followed by a team meeting in front of the board to discuss their progress on the 3 metrics.

These team meetings were critical. I needed the team managers to create habits with their team to keep everyone focused on improving these metrics.

By having the team meetings in front of the board, there was an element of peer pressure. Each team wanted to improve their metrics in order to look good for the other teams. They also started looking at the other team's metrics and started realizing that their team's actions also impacted the other department's metrics too!

The final thing the teams were required to do was to make note of the experiments they would run in the next month in an attempt to improve each metric.

Failure was ok, but lack of effort was not an option.

Ultimately, this process took on a life of its own.

My twins came home from school one day and showed me a mind map that they had created in class. The mind map was simple. In the middle circle was a concept that was linked to

3-4 smaller circles with sub concepts, that then branched out even further. I introduced this concept to my team of managers and suggested that they could use a similar approach to make connections between our teams.

As the managers started to make connections between their departments, they became more excited, and started hosting weekly meetings every Friday in our main conference room. Each week a different team would draw their mind map on a flip chart and post it on the wall in the conference room. On Friday, they would present their process to anyone else who wanted to attend, and the other teams would use yarn and tape to make connections between their processes.

After several weeks, our conference room looked like chaos, but it was fantastic! People were engaging with each other to make connections between their processes, and improvements started to come naturally and rapidly. The Friday meetings were engaging, fun, and literally standing room only. We had people in the hallways, and the best part: **I had nothing at all to do with them.** The team had taken ownership and was acting without me... **This was the start of leading instead of managing!**

Imagine how my health improved, how much more engaged my team was, and how well the processes were performing.

It was time for me to move on, and Rizza was promoted to take over the role that I left when I moved back to the USA. I am so proud of her and the team that I left behind.

Some leaders rose to the challenge, and others did not. I had to make some difficult decisions with good people in order to help some of them seek new opportunities where they could succeed, but overall, almost all of the teams rose to the challenge!

This was the impact of PEOPLE engaging with PROCESS in a positive way!

When you have the right leaders, in the right seats, with aligned metrics that monitor where you are (current state) and guide you to where you are going (future state), this is the beginning of an outstanding trajectory into your future. Tips on Quality, Value, and Speed. Each metric can be looked at internally (business focused) and externally (customer or supply chain focused)

Quality

Internal quality problems may be causing employee frustration, rework, and other problems similar to the examples provided earlier in this chapter.

Externally, quality problems may cause you lost customers, returns, and bad reviews resulting in future lost sales. Some quality problems are difficult to uncover and quantify but may be having a significant impact to your bottom line.

Value

Internal value metrics are often cost related. For example, if your internal costs are higher than they should be in order to create a profitable and sustainable organization. The internal value should also be clearly aligned with the purpose of your organization.

External value metrics are often focused on things such as revenue or purchasing costs. The more important and deeper perspective should include the value created for customers and the impact of lower cost purchased items on internal processes.

Speed

Speed can be considered the be the time it takes to complete a task. Understanding the speed impact of individual processes on the overall performance of the product/service you offer is important to creating an efficient process flow.

The interaction of internal process steps includes inventory, transportation distance, motion waste, overprocessing, and waiting time.

Internal speed metrics can help to hold accountability of your team members in order to align processes for efficiency and effectiveness.

External speed metrics impact your client delivery, and likely satisfaction. In our current society of 140-character texts and 1-minute videos, people expect rapid responses.

Reflection Questions - Engaging Your Team

1. What are some opportunities for improvement that can be aligned better within your organization?

2. Why is it so effective to have your team come up with the experiments to improve?

3. How would you rate your team's Tools, Skills, and Mindset to implement this program?

Chapter 7

The Cone of Purpose

Such are the paths of all who go after ill-gotten gain; it takes away the life of those who get it (Proverbs 1:19).

Focusing on values and purpose will enhance the lives of your leadership team and your employees. If you are in business solely for the purpose of materialism and financial gain, then your organization will burn out.

The nose cone of the rocket ship points in the direction that the organization is heading. It is designed as a cone to reduce friction, or resistance from outside forces, while it efficiently cuts through the atmosphere.

Like many people, my career has been a journey of exploration. As a Christian husband, father, leader, brother, son, and friend, I have not always made the right decisions. I have learned from my mistakes along the way and continue to grow from them. My purpose in life is clear to use my God given talents to be a positive influence in the world. Part of my story has been the growing clarity around personal and organizational purpose in life.

Early in my career, with degrees in Chemistry and Finance, I had intentions of solving the world's problems through process. Very quickly, I started to realize that process alone would not get me very far.

One of my clients (Warren) looked at me one day and said "I have been working on this machine for longer than you have been alive!" Clearly, my presumption that Process => Performance was not going to work... I needed to change my equation, and get people on board!

A key learning is that Process is only effective to the extent that People are willing to engage with it.

My equation became People + Process => Performance, and the interesting thing that I started to learn was that how

People interact with Processes in their lives are what we know as Habits.

Performance is an outcome of our Habits! Maybe not profound, but certainly a step in the right direction. The question at this point becomes... What compels People to be willing to change or adapt to a new Process?

The answer is Purpose.

The tip of the Rocket Ship is Purpose, because without it, nothing changes! When People don't have a compelling reason (Purpose) to change, then habits remain the same, and so does the outcome.

Purpose of the rocket ship relates to every other element of the model and should align your organization for the best possible result.

Purpose and Product must align well together in order for people to believe that you really believe in your purpose. I have been personally challenged with this in my life and organization. I have been presented with opportunities that fall outside of the values we have set for our organization:

1. Lead with transparency and honesty.

2. Create more value than we extract.
3. Develop long term relationships.
4. Accept failure, acknowledge it, learn from it, adapt.

I have been challenged with opportunities that would have created significant value for EPS Zone, but at the expense of the client, rather than of mutual benefit. Turning down business is never easy, but demonstrating values alignment between purpose and product is essential to long term success!

Purpose and Performance must also be aligned. If the purpose of your organization is focused on creating value for customers in order to impact your community, then your performance metrics should reflect that. Performance metrics focused only on revenue and employee costs would not be congruent with the stated purpose of the organization. Imagine being an employee of the company reading the company purpose and values, but then being evaluated based on very different criteria.

There is no doubt that all organizations must bring in enough revenue and contain costs to the extent that fulfill the organization's purpose. It is ok to clearly articulate this in context, but equally important to ensure the alignment is clear and supported by the metric definitions.

The alignment of Purpose and People is helpful to ensure that the people in your organization are a cultural fit and support your organization's purpose. I have worked with a variety of organizations, and find the unique DNA of each is important for overall success. Diversity of your team is critical for many reasons but having a common set of beliefs and purpose of overall direction is essential to success.

Process alignment is the final element, and foundational to the success of your mission.

The following beliefs will enable the success of your organization:

- Believe in where you are going and why
- Believe in the product you are selling
- Believe that your performance data will guide great decisions
- Believe in your people to deliver results
- Believe in your processes to enable your team to succeed

Lack of strong belief in any of the five elements above will make your journey a huge challenge! Which of these beliefs do you struggle with? Do you have a compelling purpose that you and your team strongly believe in?

Purpose comes in many forms that may be either intrinsic or extrinsic. Some of the factors that contribute to an individual's view of Purpose include: Faith, Family, Legacy, Survival, etc. These can be influenced by where you were born, who your parents were, how many siblings you have, your peers, your first job, and the church or school you attended as a child.

- Where do you want to go and why? The is your long-term purpose.
- What do you do today and why? This is what we call your "product" or current state purpose.

The gap between current and future state requires true leadership in order to succeed, in addition to providing clarity of purpose to be shared throughout the entire team.

One other important consideration around Purpose… As human beings, we are uniquely created to seek and fulfill purpose in our lives by impacting the lives of others. Through my work with a variety of business leaders, I have found that many Christian business leaders are conflicted with balancing the concepts of "contentment vs. greed" with a desire to "impact the world for Christ".

If you bear with me for a moment, I would like to share some wisdom about purpose that I have learned through research of history in the Bible. Below are a few verses for you to consider:

- *"Godliness with contentment is great gain"* 1 Timothy 6:6
- *The love of money is the root of all evil* (1 Timothy 6:10).
- *A slack hand causes poverty, but the hand of the diligent makes rich* (Proverbs 10:4).
- *But remember the Lord your God, for it is he who gives you the ability to produce wealth...*(Deuteronomy 8:18).

How does one reconcile these Biblical concepts which seem to conflict by encouraging both contentment and also diligent work?

$$\text{Godliness with Contentment} = \frac{(Wisdom) \times (Acts\ of\ Obedience)}{(Materialism)}$$

The wisdom of Proverbs teaches us that there are basic foundational truths to becoming leaders and growing wealth. We can and should seek wisdom and act obediently in impacting the world in a positive way.

There are two primary principles to be learned:

1. *Materialism drains humans and makes us empty.*
2. *Wisdom and Acts of Obedience enable growth*!

This does not mean you are guaranteed success by following the principles, but it is the right way to live for the right reasons!

Pirates may end their life with great financial wealth, but at what cost? Remember the verse we started this chapter with:

> *Such are the paths of all who go after ill-gotten gain; it takes away the life of those who get it.*
> (Proverbs 1:19)

As a true leader, we demonstrate servant leadership through seeking of wisdom and acting on it, rather than seeking materialism and greed. Managing the resources, we have been entrusted with is an act of obedience. Our teams will ultimately observe and feel our purpose - What is yours?

Reflection Questions About Purpose:

1. What is your Purpose? (Why do you do what you do?)

2. What is your Organization's Purpose? (Why does your organization do what they do?)

3. How well aligned are your personal purpose and the purpose of your organization?

Chapter 8

Human Energy is the Fuel that Propels Your Ship

Servant leadership includes the understanding and humility to lead our teams towards a positive outcome by caring for each person as an individual worthy of our investment to help grow.

Do nothing from selfish ambition or conceit, but in humility count others more significant than yourselves. – Philippians 2:3

There are three conditions

1. High levels of engagement of your team drive high performance.

2. Low levels of engagement of your team drive low performance

3. Imbalanced levels of engagement cause your ship to veer off course, leading to difficulty controlling the overall results.

- Your team knows when the organization's purpose is not clear. They can feel when your leadership lacks clarity around the future, the current state, and a strategy for getting to where you need to go.

- Your team knows when your metrics are misaligned, broken, missing, or pointing you in the wrong direction.

- Your team knows when your leadership team is misaligned, missing key roles, and lacking focus on a common goal.

- Your team knows when processes are broken. Giving them communication or personality training without process is putting a band-aid on a gaping wound.

This is not to say that one is more important than the other, but rather to create clarity in how all of the elements work together. When your team knows that something is wrong, their level of engagement and energy sputters out. In order to create a thriving organization, leaders must identify blind spots around the elements of success in the P^5 Rocket Ship Model.

Observation of your team's habits and behaviors is a highly effective method of understanding the energy that your team is bringing!

I recently was approached by the CEO of a rapidly growing organization to help engage his team. I asked him the question I often ask about tools, skills, and mindset. He confidently told me that they hired highly qualified individuals (skills) and provided them with the technology to do their jobs very successfully (tools). His concern was that his team simply didn't take initiative to "get stuff done"!

I followed up with a risky question... "Did you hire unmotivated candidates as employees, or have they become disengaged over time?" This was risky for me to ask, but critical for any leader to self-reflect on.

"Leaders should become concerned when motivated employees become disengaged."

If he answered that he hired unmotivated employees, this would indicate his weakness as a hiring manager
If he answered that he hired good people, but they no longer have the mindset to succeed and grow, then it would indicate a poor culture or distrust in leadership.

Either way, the responsibility for the employee disengagement of employees falls back on leadership!

Lack of trust is a key reason that employees become disengaged over time. I have seen trust described in 3 key elements found in the graphic on the next page:

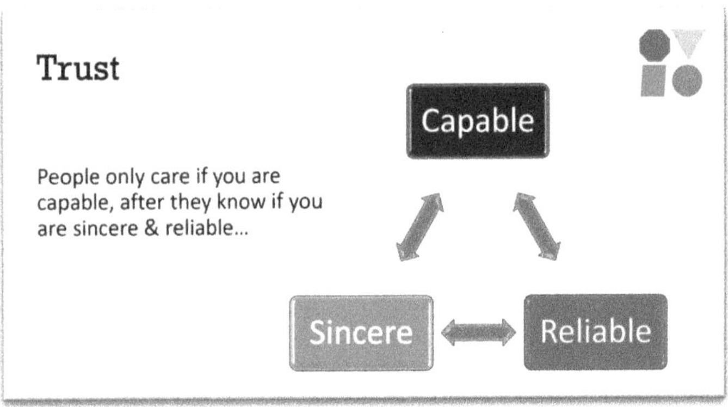

It is important to note, that people only care if you are capable, after they know if you are sincere and reliable... All three of these elements are important:

- Does your team believe you are sincere? In other words, do they believe you care about them?
- Does your team believe you are reliable? In other words, can they rely on you to do what you say?
- Finally, do they believe you are capable of executing on commitments?

The same questions can be asked of you about your employees. Do you trust your employees in each of the 3 elements, or have they broken your trust? In either case, you need to establish and execute on a plan to build trust and grow employee engagement.

A good friend, Dr. Dave NieKamp, PsyD shared with me the 4 types of relationships. Defining which of these relationships you have with your employees becomes an important factor in your ability to build trust and influence positive outcomes with emotional intelligence. The four types of relationships are defined in the following way:

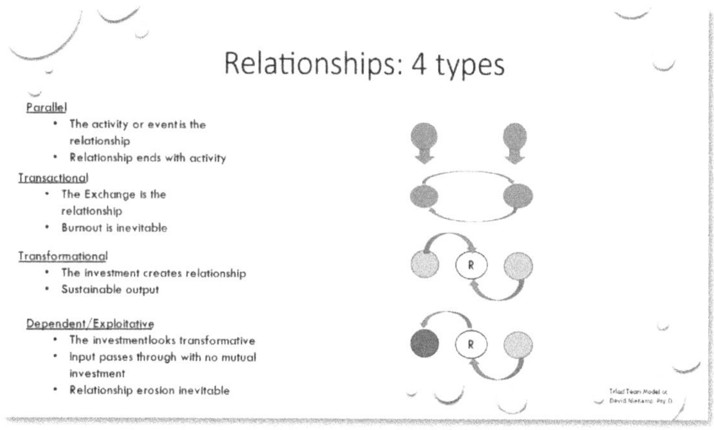

The more efficient, productive, and consistent the relationship is, the quicker trust is established, maintained and develops.

Either not understanding or knowing which type of relationship is expected and/or necessary, will lead to misunderstanding of activities and the order of those activities; ultimately creating a culture of distrust.

The better you and your employee view and understand what type of relationship is necessary for the completion of the project, the better aligned the activities will be in accordance with desired outcomes.

How you and your employee each view your relationship becomes the foundation on which you can establish and build trust!

What are you doing as a LEADER to engage your employees? How do you ensure your employees have opportunities to grow and learn?

On of the questions I ask most of the teams I work with is: "How do you prefer to learn?"

I ask this for a couple of reasons.

First, in order to grow, it is critical for individuals to learn. Without learning, there is no growth, and good leaders do NOT assume that others prefer to learn the same way as you do!

Secondly, I have become increasingly aware of the diversity in preferred learning methods within groups. This diversity in preferences is important to understand, especially if we are going to effect change for larger teams or groups of people!

Below is an example of the diversity of preferences within a recent team of people:

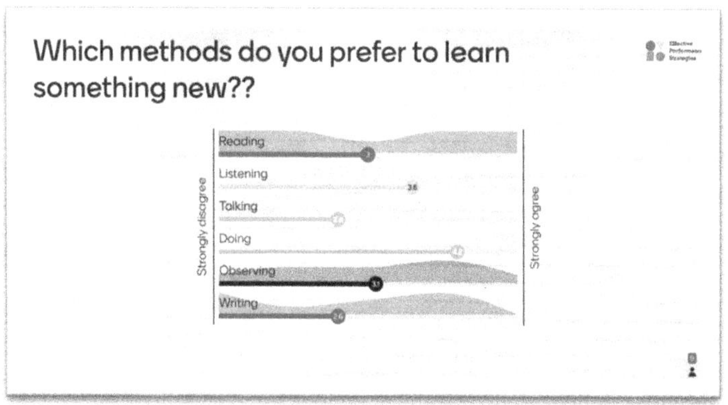

You can see within the 9 respondents, the highest preference was to "learn by doing", but there is great diversity in how the people prefer to learn! Some people rated reading as a 5, while others rated reading as a 1. If the leader of a team loves reading and assumes their team loves it to, there will be several team members who will disengage and not grow.

There is one other consideration as you navigate the human energy that propels your ship. I recently learned of 7 C's as a framework for employee fit. The 7 C's below will help as you evaluate the potential fit of candidates, and most of them remain relevant throughout the course of their employment with your organization. You can use the following questions to uncover potential areas of concern with individuals in your organization:

Calling - Why are they part of your organization?

Character - How strong is their character in the face of adversity?

Chemistry - How well do they fit with the team or organization?

Competency - How capable are they of performing the job they are currently in?

Condition - How fit are they in terms of physical, spiritual, emotional, and mental energy to perform the job?

Commitment - How committed are they to following through?

Consistency - How well do they demonstrate success consistently across

Are there folks within your team who might be in the wrong role? They may be draining the energy from their team or your entire organization due to a misalignment in one of the areas outlined above.

Considering your process of recruitment to bring new people into your organization, you may want to consider these 7 C's in recruiting, and ensuring you have the right people in the right seats.

This can have a dramatic impact on the energy propelling your organization in the right direction!

Reflection Questions About Human Energy

1. If you have a human energy problem within your organization, did you hire the wrong people, or has your team become disengaged over time?

2. If trust is lacking, what can you do to transform and rebuild relationships with your team?

3. What steps will you take to improve employee engagement within your organization?

Chapter 9

Can you see your cage?

Your first challenge is to understand the cage that you are in. In my first visit to a large manufacturing plant, I was informed by management that they wanted to increase the pounds of product being produced by a department.

There are essentially three ways to increase throughput of good products on a machine:

1. Increased Speeds (Make the machine run faster.)
2. Reduce Downtime (Keep the machine running.)
3. Eliminate Waste (Don't make bad product.)

Management believed that increasing the line speeds would negatively impact the quality, and they were already addressing quality issues on certain products. This left us with only one option: Keep the machine running more.

We initiated an exercise with a cross-functional team using a Lego® set with predefined tasks for each of the team members to replicate a process. Throughout the course of the exercise, I made analogies to their process, and provided the team with training and tools that we then used in evaluating the real process in their manufacturing plant.

On the second day of the event, we observed the process, and learned a very important fact while viewing the equipment. The brakes on the dryers had not been used for over 10 years! My eyes were open to the fact that people can walk by something that seems so obvious without seeing the cage.

The team found that some machines had missing brake pads, some operators did not even know that the brakes existed, and when the brakes were activated on the machine we chose for the exercise, brake fluid immediately started leaking from the dry rotted hoses.

Imagine for a moment that in over a decade, the operators had not used the brakes because the maintenance team told them they would wear out. Do you hesitate from using the brakes on your car because they might wear out? Imagine the safety hazard that would be created if this was part of the decision process you went through to stop at a light, or for a child running after a ball. Now consider the safety hazard of equipment in a large manufacturing plant doing the same.

The downtime reduction on the dryers ultimately unlocked several million dollars of additional capacity, and safety was dramatically improved.

In this example, the tools were Legos, but the skill was to use them to create a "safe environment" where employees could relate and open up. In the end, it was about changing a long-held mindset about whether or not to use the brakes.

Mindset (the ability to see the cage and the desire to get out) is the third critical piece. Which of these are you struggling with today? What cage may exist around you and your team that you are failing to be aware of, identify clear alternatives to, or take decisive action on?

As a leader, there are 3 imperatives for you to engage and grow your team:

1. Become aware and create awareness for your team about broken or dysfunctional processes.

2. Identify alternative options of how to engage your team in solving the process problems.

3. Make decisions and act with consistency of purpose, supporting your team in execution.

This book has provided you with two of the three elements necessary to create the roadmap for your organization to become the rocket heading toward the green planet. As you may recall, the three components were Tools, Skills, and Mindset. Each of the elements has included a template for you to complete (Tools) and recommendations for the process to complete them effectively (Skills).

In order for your team to succeed, you will need to set the cadence, hold your team accountable, and provide the leadership (Mindset) to succeed. Best wishes on your journey towards success!

Templates

You can access a variety of templates for taking a deeper dive into these topics by visiting **www.P5Rocket.com** or **contacting ryan@epszone.com to learn more!**

- **TSM: Tools, Skills, Mindset**
- **P5E: Strategy Document**
- **BSA: Blind Spot Assessment**
- **POPA: Personal and Organizational Purpose Alignment**
- **PFG: Customer Journey Map w/Pain, Fear, Gain**
- **QVS™: Quality, Value, Speed**
- **AM: Accountability Matrix and 7C's**
- **Learning Styles Assessment**
- **PM: Process Map w/Swim Lanes or Job Breakdowns**
- **EVA: Engagement Values Alignment**
- **RACI: Action Log**

About the Author

Ryan Weiss is a Christian, Husband, Father, Son, Brother, and Friend to many. He is passionate about engaging with business leaders who are interested in influencing the world in a positive way, and has over 20 years of success leading teams, programs, and operations to drive business results and profitability.

He is an accomplished executive leader with entrepreneurial spirit backed by proven ability to deliver superior business results across industries, with a strong appreciation for diverse cultures gained through extensive international work experience in more than 20 countries.

He held various global executive positions with a large consumer product and industrial adhesive company across a wide variety of functions, including finance, technical, business development, continuous improvement, and two expat assignments.

He has worked directly with customers in both manufacturing and service industries, including Chemicals, Finance, Technology, Packaging, Food, Diapers, Distribution, General Contracting, Marketing, Branding, Food Service, and Landscaping.

Ryan has also spent time managing large scale operations for major multinational organizations. He has trained thousands of people globally in continuous improvement, while keenly observing processes, cultures, and behaviors.

This broad experience has allowed him to establish a common set of themes that work across all organizations!

Acknowledgements:

Rebecca, my loving wife, for her support and encouragement as we have moved around the world, and taking the risk to start out on my own 6 years ago.

My children (Kaitlyn, Kenton, Ethan, and Emma) as we moved several times globally to grow professionally and learn about global cultures.

My parents for providing a loving home as I was growing up and challenging me to start my first business at 16 years old, setting a great foundation.

Rizza Aquino who asked the question that changed my life.

Elaine Kunkle who gave me an incredible opportunity to grow, and shared wisdom I will never forget.

Brian Wagner for his mentoring and encouragement to take the risk and spread my wings to fly.

Ed Breclaw, Jay Curtis, Dennis Drummond, and others who reviewed the book, and provided insights/feedback to make it so much better!

Megan Robinson for coaching and challenging me to complete this project with both quality and efficiency, and to jump start the marketing.

Brian Basilico (The BACON guy) who helped me refine the catchy book title and clarify the purpose.

Tony Drummond and Audrey Catapang who both work tirelessly in the background getting everything done.

Lance Bell, Bill Molinari, and Joe Slawek for encouraging me to be transparent in how my faith impacts my personal and professional life.

All of our customers who have trusted me with the opportunity to learn and grow together.

Faith, which has provided me with clarity and purpose to move beyond the materialism to make a positive impact on the world.

Family, Friends, and Collaborators (too many to mention by name) who have stood by us and impacted me in various ways over the years.

CPSIA information can be obtained
at www.ICGtesting.com
Printed in the USA
BVHW060842160222
629186BV00018B/535

9 781506 907215